# DIAMONDS EVERYWHERE

## ERNEST A. FITZGERALD

Abingdon Press
Nashville

DIAMONDS EVERYWHERE

*Copyright © 1983 by Abingdon Press*

Second Printing 1983

**Library of Congress Cataloging in Publication Data**

FITZGERALD, ERNEST A.
    Diamonds everywhere.
    1. Methodist Church—Sermons. 2. Sermons, American. I. Title.
BX8333.F53D5        1983        252'.076        82-24311

**ISBN 0-687-10734-2**

MANUFACTURED BY THE PARTHENON PRESS AT
NASHVILLE, TENNESSEE, UNITED STATES OF AMERICA

# DIAMONDS EVERYWHERE

To the
Staff and Members of
West Market Street United Methodist Church
Greensboro, North Carolina.

# In Appreciation

Like invisible fingers the magic waves of radio reach out to touch people in every nook and corner of the earth. To be afforded the facilities of "The Protestant Hour" is a privilege given only to a few. Such an opportunity must not be taken lightly. Countless people give so much of themselves to make these broadcasts possible. To all of those talented people I owe an incalculable debt.

A special word of gratitude must be given to those who have helped me so much:

To Dr. David Abernathy, a treasured friend, whose vast knowledge of communications gives him an unrivaled reputation in the field. To learn from him is a priceless experience that every speaker and writer should have;

To William Horlock and the staff of The Protestant Radio and Television Center in Atlanta, whose tireless work and excellence give "The Protestant Hour" a worldwide reputation;

To Mrs. David W. Lewis, whose technical knowledge and counsel always make writing a pleasant and rewarding effort;

To Mrs. Burt S. Eldridge, Jr., at West Market Street Church, Greensboro, whose boundless energies and skills helped make this manuscript possible;

To Mrs. Walter E. Johnston, who has the special talent of making complex ideas understandable;

To Fisher-Harrison, Inc., publishers of *Pace* magazine, who gave me permission to reprint some of the material appearing in my regular column there;

And most of all, I owe a debt to my wife, Frances, who refuses to let me be discouraged and reminds me daily to look for the "diamonds" where I am.

St. Paul's words, "I am a debtor," have a special meaning for me.

Ernest A. Fitzgerald
Greensboro, North Carolina

# Foreword

————◆————

The most intense search of our times is the quest for life—real life. Unfortunately, far too few of us find it. For many people each day is a day of dread, and living is nothing more than a monotonous grind. These people believe that if life is to have any meaning, it must be found in a place other than where they are.

The grand message of the Bible is that life can be an exciting adventure. God intended it to be that way. We can find that life where we are and regardless of our circumstances. That's what this book is about. The chapters in it constitute the basis for my broadcasts on the United Methodist Series of "The Protestant Hour" beginning in August, 1983. It is the author's hope that in these pages and through the broadcasts someone will find the dawn of a new day.

# Contents

———•———

# DIAMONDS EVERYWHERE

# Chapter 1

# DIAMONDS
# EVERYWHERE

*Do you ever feel that you don't have what it takes to
live successfully—that other people are having a better
go at life than you are? You may be missing some
things so close to you that you just don't see them.
There is a way to make life an exciting adventure.
Read Matthew 25:14-18.*

One of the best-known addresses in nineteenth-
century America was Russell Conwell's famous
lecture entitled "Acres of Diamonds." Mr. Conwell
made this address six thousand times and earned
from it more than five million dollars. He used the
money from this one lecture to endow the famous
Temple University. The theme of his lecture was that
opportunity lurks in everyone's backyard, that
everyone can and ought to find wealth and use these
riches for the good of humankind.

I have always been intrigued by that lecture for
several reasons. To imagine that the same man could
make the same speech six thousand times is
impressive and perhaps has no parallel in history.
But the thing that interests me most in this address

is its theme: opportunity *does* lurk in everyone's backyard.

If I had to make one guess about why so many of us find life meaningless, it would be that we do not feel we have what it takes to live successfully. There never seems to be enough of anything to meet the demands that are laid upon us. We have occupations that often seem to require more skills than we possess; we have more duties than time permits, and more burdens than we have strength to carry. As a result we often feel overwhelmed.

One of the best-known stories in the Bible is the story Jesus told called "The Parable of Investments." Like all of his parables, it is a simple narrative; yet, it is profound in its implications.

According to this parable there was a businessman who decided to take a trip. We don't know the nature of his business except that possibly it was a sort of investment enterprise. The man had three associates with whom he left his fortune. To these men he parceled out his holdings. To one, he gave $50,000 in silver; to another, $20,000; and to still another $10,000. He instructed the men to invest this money for an appropriate return.

When the businessman returned from his travels, he called in his associates for a report. The two men who had received extensive holdings had invested their resources wisely. The third man who had received $10,000 reported that he had simply kept what was given to him without increasing its value.

His lack of imagination cost him dearly. He lost the money and his position as well.

The parable of investments is one of the most quoted stories in literature. Volumes of sermons have been written on this parable. Most of the sermonizing, however, has dealt with the *judgment* of life about the improper use of one's possessions, wealth, or talents. All of this is valid. But I want to talk about the fellow who received the smallest amount of money. I want us to think about what he missed.

The most obvious thing, I suppose, is that he lacked a proper appreciation for what he had and that makes him a kindred spirit with many of us. Someone needs to write a book on the theme "Is It Wrong to *Love Yourself?*" Self-love or pride has always been numbered among the deadly sins, but humility has always been noted as a virtue. When Jesus gave us the Golden Rule, he said: "You shall love your neighbor as yourself." This means in effect that to love others, we must first love ourselves. Apparently, Jesus is saying that proper appreciation of oneself is *not* a sin but a necessary prerequisite to every other human association.

This sense of self-appreciation is lacking in many people. How it has happened, I don't fully understand. But it seems more obvious now than ever before. Perhaps it has to do with a culture bent on worshiping the mighty, the colossal, and the spectacular. Success appears to be whatever makes the biggest splash and accumulates the most power. We constantly measure ourselves against such criteria. A lot of us spend our lives measuring our abilities and our talents against those of more gifted people. We never recognize that the people we consider to be more gifted is a value judgment *we* ourselves make. But that value judgment may not be valid.

We also have a curious way of establishing who the really gifted people are. I have a friend named Jim who has more abilities than you can imagine. He has an excellent mind, the eye of an artist, a perfectly magnificent appearance, and a remarkably wonderful speaking voice. But this fellow has one problem: he can't seem to finish anything.

I have another friend named Tom whose abilities are far less varied, but he has the persistence of a trained bird dog. Time and again I have heard these two fellows characterized. People talk about Jim and his talents with great admiration, but they call old Tom a "plodder" as if something were wrong with him. But I wonder, isn't persistence a talent of value too? Indeed, it may be even more valuable than all the rest.

I know a lot of people like old Tom, and many of them are pretty miserable. They have been made to feel that what they have is inadequate or at least not important.

That feeling has been fostered in many ways. We have a world that values things more than it does people. It worships power more than peace and success more than righteousness. This attitude has even been found in parents who project impossible dreams for their children, wanting them to be extensions of themselves rather than the unique individuals they were meant to be. There are so many things in this world that make you believe you are totally unnecessary and what you have is either the wrong thing or is not enough. That's why many of us are so miserable. We are troubled over the insignificance of our lives.

One of the reasons this parable of the investments is so important is that it speaks to our feelings of insignificance. The parable reminds us of something that could change our lives.

It reminds us that our talents are gifts the size of which we did not determine. There is nothing in the parable to suggest that the men asked for anything. They simply took what was given to them. Isn't this essentially true about life? All of us have abilities for which we can claim no credit. For example, the person who has a quick mind in chemistry is seldom able to claim credit for it any more than the fellow who is slow in chemistry can be blamed for being dumb. Also we mostly inherit our physical features.

I don't claim to understand why there are differences among us, but I do know that many of us boast of talents for which we can claim no credit at all. We have a way of putting down people who seem to have fewer talents. Yet they are not at all responsible for their limitations. To some degree all of our abilities are gifts from God, and we have no right to boast of or belittle what God has given us.

How we use what we have is more important than what we have.

I once read a story about Abraham Lincoln. The truth of it I cannot verify. But true or not, its lesson *is* true to life. During the Civil War, General Sherman was sent with his army to carry out a strategic mission. For some reason Sherman stood idle for days and did nothing. Lincoln, in his own subtle way, became impatient and sent Sherman a message. He said, "General, if you are not going to use your army, do you mind if I borrow it? We have a war going on." Lincoln's point is clear. A little talent used is better than a lot of talent never used.

It is also true that a little effort used in the proper place is more effective than a lot of effort in the wrong place. You balance a tire on your automobile with only a few ounces of lead—not with a ton of weight. So much of the world is changed by people with a talent totally invested, while people, much more capable, live and die and achieve nothing.

I look back at my life, and I remember all kinds of people who have touched me. I see brilliant people who helped me on my way: professors whose memories were packed with a wealth of information, skilled people who grasped the deepest problems of my life and provided invaluable assistance. But I remember folk like old Tom who didn't have much to offer except determination. They made it easier for me when the going was tough and helped me over some hurdles I might not have made without their help. I'd be hard pressed today to determine which people have been of greater value to me—the brilliant people or the slow and steady people.

History has often depended on the people who could do little else but be persistent: a soldier in a ditch waiting for the master strategist to arrive, an innkeeper in Bethlehem who found a warm stable in which a Child could be born, or even a man who helped carry a cross to a faraway hillside in Jerusalem two thousand years ago.

Who really knows which people are important? Life could be richer for us if we spent less time trying to measure up to someone else and more time using what we have. There are acres of diamonds in our own backyards. All we have to do is look for them and use them.

*PRAYER:* Eternal God, forgive us for our failure to appreciate who we are and what you have given us. Remind us that despite our limitations we have received greater blessings than we sometimes realize. Give us discerning minds and hearts that we may discover the precious diamonds you have placed in our own backyards. And when we have found them, help us use them so we can find the life you intended us to have. Amen.

# Chapter 2

—◆—

# HOMEMADE DIAMONDS

*Do we really appreciate our families? This God-given social unit offers countless opportunities for life's most priceless experiences. Our loved ones are the most important people in our lives. Think of the treasures our families can bring to us.*
*Read I Corinthians 13:4-7.*

A few years ago a Texas churchman wrote a book that received wide acclaim in the religious circles of our land. In that book, *A Second Touch,* Keith Miller wrote about an humbling experience which occurred in his home. One morning Miller got up early for his daily prayer and Bible study. As he was struggling with his lesson, one of his children interrupted and asked what he was doing reading *that book.* Irritated at the interruption, Miller told his daughter to be quiet and get out of the room. A moment later he heard the little girl, sniffling back her tears, asking her mother, "What's the matter with Daddy?" "Oh," replied Miler's wife, "he is learning how to be a good Christian so he can love the people *downtown.*"

Many of us can relate to that experience. Sometimes the people we hurt the most are those who are the closest to us. We are kind and courteous to our friends and neighbors, but with our loved ones we often are rude and impatient. We have time for all sorts of activities with the people downtown, but so frequently we are strangers to our families.

Many years ago Henry Grady, the great southern newspaper editor, said that the heart of America is the home. Grady's intent, no doubt, was to extol the sanctity of marriage and the sacred trust of parenthood. But there is another meaning here.

The most precious possession you can ever have is the love of your family. In this God-given social unit are countless opportunities for some of life's greatest experiences. If we could understand how important our loved ones really are, our appreciation for them would take on new dimensions.

Centuries ago the apostle Paul wrote a letter to some of his friends. In his letter is a section which must be included in the greatest passages of literature. Paul describes the true nature of love. Among other things, he makes this observation: "Love bears all things, . . . hopes all things, endures all things." What do you suppose would happen if those qualities were present in our homes?

First, Paul is saying that love *bears* all things. A few weeks ago the children in a church school class were asked to copy the thirteenth chapter of I Corinthians from their Bibles. One little girl misread a phrase and wrote, "Love shares all things." While the girl's translation may not be faithful to the

24

original language, her thought was accurate. It is the spirit of sharing that makes the home a blessed and sacred place.

One of the loveliest stories in the Bible is found in the biography of Samuel. Samuel came from a modest home, but his parents had great dreams for him. One day his father and mother sent him away to a boarding school. The biblical account tells us that each year Samuel's mother went up to visit him and took him a little coat she had made. There you have it—the privilege and obligation of love. It is the spirit of sharing.

Cecil Myers reports a definition of a happy home as given by a thirteen-year-old boy: "A happy home is like a baseball team, with Mom pitching, Dad catching, the kids fielding and everyone taking a turn at bat."

The boy's analogy is not altogether bad. It applies to families with all kinds of structures—single parents, couples without children, children caring for aged parents, or relatives caring for one another. The point is that a happy family functions as a team with each member undergirding and supporting the other members. Life isn't easy for any of us, but it's far more bearable if tough times can be shared by people who care.

A few years ago an author I know dedicated one of his books to his wife. He paid her a lovely tribute. "To my wife, who has made our home a hiding place from the wind and a shelter from the storm." Can you think of any possession greater than a home such as that? Our world is a tough place in which to live. So often we feel that life is a rat race where we are pushed along in senseless and foolish directions. All of us, now and then, need some respite from the wind and the storm. Fortunate, indeed, is the person who has a loved one who can share those hard times. Our homes, if we work at it, can be a shelter.

Second, Paul reminds us that love *hopes* all things. The most overlooked resource on this earth is human potential. Years ago there was a minister at the First Congregational Church in Los Angeles. In his early years this minister was not recognized as one of the great preachers of America. Had you listed the greatest speakers of this land his name, in all likelihood, would not have been included. Later this Congregational minister's name would be remembered when most of his colleagues were forgotten. Lloyd C. Douglas became one of America's all-time best selling authors. His books *The Magnificent Obsession, The Robe,* and *The Big Fisherman* will be read for generations to come.

What a commentary on the ways of life. What we are and what we may become are seldom the same. You never know when you have a winner.

Do you suppose this is what Paul had in mind when he said, "Love hopes all things"? Hope sees the possibilities within us. Genuine love attempts to help each person realize his or her best self.

About a hundred years ago the body of a man was brought home from Africa. The man had died some thirty years before. An honor procession made its way through Washington, D. C., to a burial place established for John Howard Payne. In the procession were the President of the United States, many senators and congressmen, and a host of friends. As Payne was laid to rest, a thousand-voice choir sang a song that Payne had written. The song had been a part of a play first presented in Paris. That song, "Home Sweet Home," is said to be among the most widely known in the world. In the last stanza, Payne speaks of home as a place for peace, a place for the renewal of spirit, and a place where sagging spirits can be given new life. That's what the home can be for us. It can be a place where our loved ones help us renew our vision of what we can be. We should never treat lightly those who challenge us to become our finest and best.

Third, Paul declares that love *endures* all things. John Wesley once wrote that his mother never lost patience with her children. Not many of us can boast of a similar achievement. We do become impatient with one another. It is true, however, that of all human institutions, the family has the greatest capacity for believing, for being disappointed and believing again.

Paul may have had this in mind when he said, "Love endures all things." Love always offers a second chance. Remember the story Jesus told us about the boy who ran away from home? The lad wasted everything. One night he returned and said to his father, "Father, I have sinned. . . . I am no longer worthy to be called your son; treat me as one of your hired servants." The record is clear. The father refused the boy's request to be a servant. He made him a son again.

That quality of forgiveness is possible in every home. Not one of us is infallible. Life is a series of victories and defeats, of successes and failures, of gains and losses. If we were counted out every time we went down, life would be intolerable and impossible. All of us need someone to believe in us and to help us start again. Our families provide the finest opportunities for that. Here our ties can be the strongest if we want them to be.

A few years ago there was a popular song entitled "He Ain't Heavy, He's My Brother." That title first appeared on a small card circulated as an advertisement by a printing company. The card pictured a small boy being carried by another boy. Someone must have asked the boy if his load was too heavy. To that question the boy replied, "He ain't heavy, he's my brother." Genuine love is like that. It carries burdens without murmur or complaint.

It's a foolish person who spends all his time trying to get along only with the people downtown. Our greatest opportunities for love and affection are those with whom we live day by day. Sometimes we forget that, and like the prodigal son, we seek our comradeship with people elsewhere. Many times, however, what we really seek can be found at home.

When Admiral Byrd wrote his great book *Alone,* he told of the long months he spent in complete solitude at the South Pole. A few lines in that book are worth remembering. "At the end only two things really matter . . . the affection and understanding of [one's] family. Anything . . . else [one] creates [is] insubstantial" (*Light from Many Lamps*, Lillian Eichler Watson). Why not take a new look at the people with whom you live or with whom you share a family circle? Are there bridges that need to be rebuilt and ties that should be mended? Why not work on those bridges and ties? Love can have its deepest and best meaning in the home. Here you find people who are worth far more than diamonds.

*PRAYER:* Eternal God and Creator of us all, how glad we are for the companionship of our loved ones. What a dreadful world it would be if no one cared for us. We acknowledge that we have not always been appreciative of this priceless blessing. We have often been careless in our treatment of those closest to us. Help us now to be more sensitive to those we love and who love us. Help us see within them a spark of the divine. Let us so live together that we may realize the limitless possibilities of genuine love. In Christ's name. Amen.

# Chapter 3

————◆————

# ENVYING
# THE WRONG PEOPLE

*Many people live on the edge of despair. They are
discouraged, hopeless, and feel they have no purpose in
life. Near to all of us is an institution that addresses
these problems. The church can help us find a new life.
Read Hebrews 10:23-25.*

Several years ago the ministers of a major city
gathered at a prominent church for their annual
Christmas party. Sometime during the evening, one
of the custodians of the church found a tiny boy
standing in the hallway crying. A quick investigation revealed that the lad belonged to no one in the
building. Parking lots and properties near the church
were checked to no avail. The police were called and
within moments they sent bulletins to radio and
television stations throughout the community.

Late that evening there were reports that an
out-of-state car had stoppd at a service station north
of the city. Someone in the car asked if a boy had been
found at a downtown church; the car then disap-
peared. To my knowledge the parents of the child
were never found. The little boy has since been placed

in a splendid home where he can be reared in an atmosphere of love and care.

The morning after the little boy was found, a newsman reporting the incident began his story with this sentence: "Someone trusted the church last night, and the church came through." I sincerely hope this reporter was right. I do know that within hours the resources of a large downtown church were marshaled and placed at the lost child's disposal.

The church has come through countless times in its history. Because it has survived, its place in human affairs has been of strategic and supreme importance. I haven't always felt this way, however. My father was a minister and served small rural parishes throughout his career. He usually had a half-dozen churches on his circuit, and he insisted that his family attend all of them. I can remember leaving home on Sunday morning, and before the day was over having attended at least three services and listened to a like number of sermons. I can remember passing the homes of people who never went to church. They were preparing for picnics and outings. How I envied the boys and girls whose fathers were not ministers, whose parents never went to church.

As the years passed, I came to realize that I was envying the wrong people. It was not the folk who never went to church that deserved my envy: it was the people who did. These church people were gaining something that would be of singular importance in their lives.

The author of the Book of Hebrews must have had

this in mind when he wrote to his friends reminding them to meet together regularly. He knew his readers would find things in the community of faith that they needed. That's a thought worthy of our attention. It is possible that we, too, may discover in the church some possessions we can ill afford to be without. Think for a moment about some of our needs.

Consider, for instance, our need for strength. In *The Book of Worship of* The United Methodist Church is an old prayer which contains this sentence: "Lift our eyes above the shadows of this earth that we may see the light of eternity."

Each time I read that sentence I am reminded that it is not only a petition but also a reflection on life as it really is. The world is full of shadows; and after a while those shadows fall on each of us.

I once read about a man who shortly before World War II believed that a global conflict was coming. He decided to find a place he could be safe whatever happened. He studied a map of the world and chose one of the most remote and least populated islands on the globe. He moved there. The island turned out to be Guadalcanal, the scene of one of the bloodiest battles in human history. That man's experience is a commentary on the way life is. We struggle for security and protection only to find that there is no place to hide.

All of us are potential targets of life's eventualities. Illness, for example, is no respecter of persons. Accidents, disappointments, and failure lurk on every trail. Despite the advances in medicine, the death rate is still 100 percent. Problems and perplexities come to all of us. There *is* no place to hide. If life is to be lived at all, it must be lived in the storm.

In the Old Testament is a story of a man who must have been concerned about this. He wrote, "I would rather be a doorkeeper in the house of my God than dwell in the tents of wickedness."

We assume the author was saying that he had rather be an humble servant of God than the ruler of a kingdom. That's a part of his meaning, but not all of it. The psalmist was telling us that at the door of the temple he had found greater treasures than he might have found in the vaults of a king.

A lot of people make that discovery at the doors of the church. They find there the supportive fellowship of concerned people who have claimed God's protective promises. Remember how it was in the early church. The first Christians were considered criminals and hunted like animals. Alone in that kind of world, it was easy to lose faith. They came together, however, shared their troubles, and then encouraged one another to face whatever came. That kind of fellowship, I suppose, does not always exist in every church today. But when you find it, it is a source of strength no one can afford to miss.

We have a need, too, for hope. Dr. Ralph Sockman in his book *How to Believe* wrote an interesting sentence: "Six days a week we sit at the loom. On the seventh day God calls us to come look at the design." Days do get disconnected and the meaning of life gets

lost. Have you observed how life gets broken into bits
and pieces? We go about our daily tasks trying to do a
little good here and there. The world is so vast,
however, and our contribution seems so insignificant
that we often wonder if what we do really counts.

There is a mound of rubble in East Berlin where
once stood one of the proudest buildings in the world.
In that building, the headquarters of Hitler's Third
Reich, was a man who during the early forties was
writing his diary. The author, Joseph Goebbels, was
a brilliant man. He had been educated at the best
German universities where he earned his Ph.D. In
his diaries are several references to Mahatma
Ghandi. Goebbels considered Gandhi a fool. He
suggested that if Gandhi had had the sense to
organize militarily, he might have hoped to win the
freedom of his people.

History has made its own judgment in the matter.
Goebbel's strategy of force failed while Gandhi's
passive resistance prevailed.

Goebbels found it difficult to see the longer view,
and so do we. We struggle for a cause that's right and
good, yet it appears to fail. We give ourselves to a
noble work, believing that somewhere the seeds we
sow will come to harvest. The harvest doesn't seem to
come. It's so easy to lose heart and wonder if the bits
and pieces of our lives make any sense at all.

There are times when all of us need to take a look at
the total design. The church is one place where that
picture can be seen. The business of the church is to
remind us, as Benjamin Franklin observed, that an

Unseen Hand governs in human affairs. That Hand is determined that no good cause ever comes to a bad end. Our noble efforts are not in vain. The church has that message and all of us need to be reminded of it. No wonder the author of the Book of Hebrews said we should remember to go to church Sunday.

The church also affords us a vehicle through which we may channel our talents. I have a friend who recently faced the task of dismantling his childhood home. His father and mother had been thrifty people. They saved odds and ends of everything. Up in the attic my friend found a box, neatly closed and labeled. On the label he found these words, "Strings too short to use." "My mother and dad were wrong," said the man. "I tied those bits of string together and used them in my packing."

There is a point in this story. Not many of us are able to achieve alone what needs to be done in our world. Our meager efforts seem too limited to be useful. A lot of young people are baffled by this circumstance. There are global problems such as hunger, illiteracy, and widespread disregard for human rights. How do you get at these problems working alone? Most of us feel helpless and ineffective. As a result, many of us surrender with a deep-seated sense of insignificance.

The author of the Book of Hebrews was sensitive to this predicament. "Come together," he said to his readers, "and encourage one another in all good works." He knew that in unity there is strength. People working together can achieve what they could not accomplish working alone. That's been evident to the church for a long, long time. The servant community constitutes a part of the reason for the church's existence.

What do you have to offer in the task of building a better world? Our talents and skills differ. What one person can do, perhaps another cannot do. If somehow our efforts can be blended, together we can have an impact on what needs to be done. The church is under mandate to create that opportunity for us.

The church has not always lived up to its obligation. At times it turns in on itself and becomes detached from its environment. But always within its structure there is a remnant of those who have a vision of what the church ought to be. To the people who constitute this remnant, we can give ourselves. In doing so we accomplish at least two things: (1) we help the church remain vital, and (2) with our sisters and brothers we are able to be God's hands in the world.

What are your needs? Are you having trouble standing up to the realities of life? Do you sometimes wonder if there is any reason for your existence? Do you ever ask, "Can I make my life count?" These questions are age-old.

A long time ago the author of Hebrews wrote, "Let us hold fast . . . not neglecting to meet together." Or as we would put it today, "Go to church next Sunday." What may seem to be a useless exercise could be a time when we discover some channels that will change our lives.

*PRAYER:* Father, help us remember that life need not be a lonely voyage. You have provided places where our strength can be renewed, our spirits can find new hope and our hands can find work to do. Help us seek these places so that our lives may be exciting adventures. In our Lord's name. Amen.

# Chapter 4

———◆———

# GOD'S
# TENTMAKERS

*Do you ever feel that your daily work is a grind and
that you are accomplishing nothing of significance?
Suppose you could find a way to bring another dimension to your vocation. Honest toil can be
rewarding if we make it that way.
Read John 5:2-5, 8-9, 15-17.*

A large industry in a southern state recently engaged
a consulting firm to do a study among its employees.
One of the questions the interviewers asked was,
"Why do you work?" To the surprise of all involved,
the first response was not money. The employees
gave such answers as, "To provide for my family," "To
feel useful," "To achieve recognition," or "To be with
other people." The consulting firm concluded that
money is not the chief interest of most people seeking
work. The majority of the people interviewed seemed
to be looking for their place in the sun.

It would be easy to misinterpret the discoveries of
this study. To imagine that compensation is inciden-
tal to human behavior would be a mistake. While it is
true that money is not the overriding concern of most

people, we do expect something to result from the things we do. Most psychologists insist that we never do anything without some expectation of a return, and that every act, every word, is calculated to produce a reward.

It is this desire for compensation, we assume, that drives us to our daily tasks. We climb out of bed, dress quickly, grab a fast breakfast, and dash off to the job. Our work may be in a factory, in an office, or in the home. We may travel, sit at a desk, or operate a machine. In any event, most of us have a vocation; and we like to believe that what we do brings us some reward.

For some people, however, work provides no sense of accomplishment.

Twenty-seven centuries ago the prophet Isaiah described some folk he knew in this fashion: "In the morning they wish it were evening. In the evening they wish it were morning." Today countless people view their lives in a similar manner. They work at tasks they do not enjoy and they see no way of escape. Their jobs are dull and uninteresting. They while away the time counting the days left until retirement. Many of these people ask themselves, "Is there any way for me to find some satisfaction from the work I do?" That question has no easy answer.

Can we find some insight into this matter of satisfaction by examining the ways we view our work? Consider three possibilities.

Some people, for instance, see their work as a curse. In the first chapter of Genesis is the account of

Adam and Eve and their fall. Adam and Eve were disobedient to the instructions given them as they were placed in the garden. As a result, they were driven out and were told that thereafter they could live only by the "sweat of their brows." It is possible to misunderstand this story and believe that work is punishment because of our disobedience to God.

Remember, however, that Jesus said, "My Father works and I must work." When you examine the total message of the Bible, especially the teachings of Jesus, work is not considered a punishment. Instead, it is understood as a blessing. H. C. Ferree, the noted news columnist, tells a story of a man who accidentally touched off an explosion and blew himself to pieces.

When he came to in the hereafter, he looked around and said: "I'm going to like it here. Things are simply wonderful. I'm glad it happened." As he sat enjoying himself, an attendant came up and asked, "Is there anything I can do for you?" The man replied, "No, I have everything I could wish for." A couple of hours later the attendnt made the same inquiry and received the same answer. The third time, however, the man was becoming restless from so little activity. "Yes," he said, "I would like to play some golf." "Sorry," said the attendant, "we have no golf course here." "Well," declared the man, "let me work in the garden." "I'm sorry," said the attendant, "but our guests are not permitted to work in the garden." "All right," replied the man, "I'll just gather some fruit." Again the attendant objected. "Oh, no, the fruit will

41

be gathered for you." The man was furious. "See here. If I am not allowed to do anything here, what's heaven for?" "Mister," said the attendant, "you're not in heaven!"

We understand the point of that parable. Someone has rightly observed that if there is anything worse than having too much to do, it's having nothing to do. There have been a few times in my life when, because of illness, complete inactivity was necessary. In those moments I began to understand how miserable life would be if I were completely helpless. Even the dullest and most routine task takes on a new meaning when you try to imagine what life would be like if there were nothing to do. Work is not a curse, but the absence of it can be!

Other people see work as a duty. In 1805 the British Navy was sent to battle the combined forces of Napoleon. The commander of the British fleet was Lord Horatio Nelson. Nelson chased the French fleet all the way from the West Indies to the coasts of Spain. On the morning of October 21, Nelson finally managed to engage in battle. He sent a message to his forces which probably earned him that monument which stands in London's Trafalgar Square. "England expects every man to do his duty!" Few warriors have fought with greater bravery.

There is no way to measure the impact that people with a sense of duty have had on history. Lon Tinkle in his book *Thirteen Days to Glory* describes those dramatic hours just preceding the fall of the Alamo. Tinkle reported that these men stayed, not because they hated life but because they loved honor more; not because they were immune to the natural urge for survival, but because they were pledged to their duty.

History is alive with examples of people driven by a sense of duty. Moses didn't go to Egypt willingly. If we can believe the Old Testament, Moses felt he was under orders. Martin Luther reluctantly took his position before the Diet of Worms. Remember his famous lines? "Here I stand, God help me, I can do no other." Many times the world has been changed because people felt they had obligations.

Never minimize the impact of people with a sense of duty. Our motivation for work, however, must be more than that. When we are driven by obligations only, we work because we must and not because we want to. We spend our time doing one thing when we had rather be doing something else. Little satisfaction is derived from our work if we work simply because it is our duty.

Also, there are people who view their work as an opportunity. Dr. Ralph Sockman told a story about a man and his invalid wife who were traveling aboard an ocean liner. The man was obedient to his wife's every command. Other passengers aboard the ship observed the quaint arrangement and commented openly about it. At last the man offered an explanation. "Years ago there was a shortage of funds at my office. Although I was innocent, I was held accountable and required to make the adjustment. My wife alone believed in me. She sacrificed everything, including her health, to enable me to clear my name. If I appear now to be her servant, let me say that no master ever had a more willing servant."

There is a lesson here. An Old Testament writer said, "I delight to do thy will, O my God." This ancient author found his work a joy because of the opportunity it gave him to express his gratitude for God's goodness. Work takes on an entirely different meaning if we can see it as an opportunity. The possibilities for that are limitless.

Through our jobs, for instance, we can render a needed service to humankind, either by the services we perform or by the products we produce. Remember, too, that it is through our work that we are able to provide for the needs of our loved ones.

Sometimes we have to use all our imagination to see the opportunities in our work. That is especially true if our jobs are dull and uninteresting. Two thousand years ago there was a man who traveled the world as a missionary for the early church. St. Paul's vocation, however, was not that of an evangelist. He was, we believe, a tentmaker, meaning a leather worker, by trade. That must have been boring and unexciting work. But Paul worked at his trade to provide himself with the necessary resources and opportuniies to do his missionary work. There is an important insight here. All of us want to feel that our lives count. We want to believe that when we have finished we have not lived in vain. Sometimes our vocations enable us to feel this way. The work we do is of special significance to our brothers and sisters.

Sometimes, however, our vocations are such that we do not have this feeling. The temptation then is to seek another job. Often that isn't possible. We are caught in what we do because of age, lack of opportunity, or need for training. In such a circumstance there is at least one recourse. We can look for ways within our vocations, or our avocations, to be of service to God and to others.

Douglas Horton tells about an old friend who showed him a factory in New Jersey. "Here," said the friend, "I served God for forty years." Aren't there ways to do that in any honorable vocation? A lot of dull and dreary work can be made far more exciting if we approach it with the question, What can I do today, where I am, to make the world a better place?

*PRAYER:* Sometimes, our Father, we feel pressured and harassed by the tasks that are before us. We struggle with these tasks only to feel that our efforts are in vain. More than anything, we want to believe that what we do has meaning. Help us, Lord, to find a way to give our daily toil significance. Let us believe that a good deed is never lost and that what we do in thy name is preserved throughout all eternity. Help us every day to find an opportunity to be of service to our brothers and sisters and to remember that as we serve them, we also serve thee. Amen.

# Chapter 5

————◆————

# BACKYARD
# GREATNESS

*Do you believe that only the most talented people can find useful and meaningful lives? That's an age-old illusion. God has arranged creation so each person's contribution can be strategic and unique. There is a way to make our lives count right where we are. Read Matthew 6:26-30.*

Recently a thirteen-year-old boy wrote a letter to a newspaper about a rumor he had heard at school. The boy asked if the sun were burning out and if the earth would soon be without heat or light.

The newspaper's editors answered that lad and underscored the staggering dimensions of our universe. They told him that the sun is a giant nuclear reactor which has been burning its hydrogen fuel for some five billion years. Someday, they told him, the sun will exhaust its supply of hydrogen and, in its waning moments, explode with sizzling temperatures. On that day the oceans will be vaporized by heat in excess of one thousand degrees. All vegetable and animal life will disintegrate. They reassured the youngster that there is no immediate cause for alarm. Unless something unforseen happens, the sun still has about five billion years to go.

As we have explored the mysteries of space, we have become increasingly aware of the size of our world. This awareness has had an interesting effect on our self-evaluation. At one time people believed themselves to be the central focus of creation. But today, our sense of self-worth has diminished. We see ourselves as finite creatures on a speck of cosmic dust in a tiny corner of an infinite universe. Add to that the recent surge in population, the growing complexity of our social structures, and you can understand why so many people wonder if the individual really counts for anything. A lot of us feel, as Harry Emerson Fosdick so aptly put it, like "a peanut in Yankee Stadium."

A long time ago, Jesus anticipated this very problem. One day as he was talking to his people, he said: "Consider the lilies of the field, . . . they toil not, neither do they spin: . . . yet . . . Solomon in all his glory was not arrayed like one of these. . . . if God so clothe the grass of the field, which today is, and to-morrow is cast into the the oven, shall he not much more clothe you?" (KJV). The primary intent of these words was to remind the people of God's infinite care for each person. There is, however, another meaning here that should not be overlooked.

In that far-off day, Jesus climbed a little hill outside the city of Capernaum. As he sat down the people gathered about him in despair. Their nation had once been a proud and prosperous land. But those glorious days were gone. Rome had spread its legions from the coast of Spain to the borders of Persia. People everywhere had been subjected to Roman domination. No longer did conquered nations have a voice in their own destiny. Rome was the final authority and Caesar was Lord. The people felt they didn't count.

Many of us can identify with those folk who gathered about Jesus on that long-ago day. We, too, feel that we have been depersonalized.

Bennett Cerf in his book *Stories to Make You Feel Better* told of a man who received a statement from a large oil company. The bill was for "zero dollars and no cents." The man ignored the bill. Notices kept coming until one day he got one labeled "Final warning. Pay in full or legal action will be taken." The man sat down and wrote a check for "zero dollars and no cents" and mailed it to the company. A few days later a letter came thanking the man for his prompt payment.

We can believe that story because we live in a computerized, mechanized, impersonalized world. We often wonder if we can have any effect at all on the system.

It was to this very feeling that Jesus directed his remarks that day. He pointed to some lilies growing nearby and reminded his hearers of God's individual care. He talked about the sparrow, the most insignificant of all the birds. "Yet," said Jesus, "not one sparrow falls but that God is present for its

49

funeral." "Now," continued Jesus, "if God cares for the lilies and the sparrows, how much more will he care for you? After all, you are his children" (paraphrase). The infinite worth of each person in God's sight—that's what the Bible is about. We are not lost in the vast reaches of creation. The psalmist said, "When I consider the heavens and the earth, I ask, 'What is man that God is mindful of him?'" (paraphrase). The psalmist then answered his own question. "God has made us a little lower than the angels and given us dominion over all he has made" (paraphrase). The New Testament declares that Jesus came for the least and last one of us. God does not see us as people. We are seen as persons. We are known one by one, and one by one we are important to God. If we could truly believe that, we would no longer feel we live without reason. Life always has meaning if you know you count for something.

We need to recover a feeling of our own significance. Far too many of us believe we are useless. We are caught in the system and nothing we do seems to make any difference. As a consequence, "we give up and drop out."

I have a friend who recently made a comment worth considering. "Nothing ever happens in the world until someone gets an idea and stays with it until it prevails."

I keep thinking about that. Great movements always start with determined individuals. The church began that way. One Man called twelve disciples. The twelve became seventy, and then hundreds. Today there are millions. That's how the church came to be. One Man had a plan and a few people helped him. They stayed with the plan until it prevailed. That message needs repeating in a world where so few people believe you can "fight city hall."

I often wish that a competent student would take time to do an in-depth study of the impact a single individual can have. In 1928 a Scottish doctor was engaged in research on influenza. One day he noticed that a strange-looking mold had developed on a culture plate. Further study revealed that the mold had created a bacteria-free circle about itself. We will never fully know the impact the discovery of penicillin has had on the world. Countless lives have been saved by it. The discovery came about through the work of Alexander Fleming, and he stumbled onto it largely by accident. Do we ever really know when a small event will make a difference in our world?

A part of our problem is that we look for the big things we can do and miss the details that can really change the life of another person. Most of us won't have the opportunity to make world-changing decisions. But all of us can be alert for a small word or deed that will touch another life. There are no useless people.

A few years ago a delightful story appeared in *Pulpit Digest* magazine. One cold winter morning a woman noticed a small boy without shoes. She took him to a store and bought him shoes and socks. The

51

boy left without a word of thanks and the woman was disturbed by his ingratitude. But in a moment the lad was back. "Lady," he said, "I forgot to thank you for my shoes, and I want to ask you a question. Are you God's wife?" The woman stumbled for an answer and then mumbled, "No, I'm just one of his children." "Well," said the boy, "I 'knowed' you was kin to him someway" (*Pulpit Digest,* May-June, 1975).

Jesus talked about this very thing a long time ago. Remember how he put it. When we give a crust of bread, a cup of water, or make a visit to a stranger, it's an act of kindness that makes us akin to God.

I keep trying to remember this as I go along. Not many of us are going to shake the world by deeds that make the headlines. Most of us will manage only a cup of water, a crust of bread, or a word of encouragement to someone in need. But if God is careful enough to see the lilies in the fields and to count the sparrows in their flight, the little things we do won't be lost.

Like seeds sown in a garden, these little things will be brought to full harvest. The fact is, we really never know when our lives count for something important. A doctor, working alone at one task, made an accidental discovery that changed the world. A woman and a pair of shoes gave a small boy a glimpse of God that the boy had never seen before.

Can we ever really say that our lives do not count? Diamonds in the form of opportunities can be found everywhere if we seek them. The truly great people are those who take these opportunities, no matter how small, and use them in the service of God and humankind.

*PRAYER:* Lord, sometimes we feel so useless and insignificant. We struggle to find our place in the sun, and yet what we accomplish seems so small. Remind us that we are your special creation and what you have made is always good. Help us see that we can so invest our lives that our labor is never in vain. There are opportunities everywhere to use what we have. Make us sensitive to these opportunities so that we may find the life that is life indeed. We pray in the name of Him who was the servant of all. Amen.

# Chapter 6

# A WORD
# FROM THE EAGLE

*Our world is on the move. One out of every seven Americans changes residence each year. Some of them are looking for the ideal environment—a place where they can be happy. Have you ever imagined that life would be better if you moved somewhere else? More often than not, that is an illusion.*
*Read Exodus 15:22, 27; 16:1-3.*

On an October day in 1957 from a site near the Caspian Sea, a 184 pound package of highly sensitive instruments was shuttled into outer space. The flight of that flying laboratory was the culmination of a dream which began centuries ago. People such as Kepler, Galileo, Copernicus, Jules Verne, and H. G. Wells had dreamed of the day when the gravitational pull of the earth could be overcome. Sputnik I proved that it could be done. With its success the race to the moon began.

Three and one-half years later, Major Yuri Gagarin made the first trip into space. On the afternoon of July 20, 1969, the world received the now-famous message, "The Eagle has landed." That message came from the moon, a quarter of a million miles out in space.

There was scarcely a person in the civilized world who heard that message without some emotion. For many people it precipitated hopes for a new world. Perhaps out there somewhere is a new planet, capable of supporting life, to which we might escape and leave behind the problems of this dirty, ravaged, strife-ridden world. That dream lurks in the minds of many. If we could only find a new world, we imagine, we might find a new life.

This solution to our difficulties has long been a dream for many people. If we could but get to a different environment, things might be better there. This thought has driven us to the four corners of the earth. We have established new colonies and adopted new sets of rules. Things seem to be better for a while, and then we are confronted with the same old ills. This collective dream is also an individual one. You hear it now and then, "If I could only go to a new place, get a new start, change environments, life would be different." For the most part that's an illusion. Things generally do not go better. Before long, life gets about as tangled in the new place as it was in the old one. We keep asking the question, "What goes wrong?"

The answer to that question is simple. We carry our problems with us. You see, we really have two difficulties: our environment and ourselves. Not enough is said about the latter problem. We focus on our circumstances rather than on our inner lives. We believe we are the victims of the system and at the mercy of our surroundings. To some degree, we are. But is it also true that no environment on the outside is right for us if we are wrong on the inside? It would seem, therefore, that somewhere along the way we need to examine our total problem. That isn't an easy assignment, but it is crucial. Unless we face the total problem, our hope of finding happiness will be short-lived.

An Old Testament story might help us here. It comes from those terrible days when the Israelites lived in Egyptian slavery. The Israelites had suffered long and painfully. One day Moses appeared before the throne of Egypt and demanded the release of his people. The struggle for independence was intense and violent, but at last the tormented Israelites were set free. They were no longer slaves. The long night of bondage was over.

Two hundred miles northeast of Egypt was an extremely fertile land called Canaan. Canaan was to be the new home for the Israelites. Between Canaan and Egypt, however, were miles and miles of rough and rugged country. Wild and desolate hills were almost devoid of trees and vegetation. Only occasionally would the rainfall be enough to provide sustenance for the flocks of nomadic shepherds. It was bad country and the Israelites felt trapped in that terrible land. Disillusioned and cynical, they registered their complaint. "Moses," they said, "did you bring us out here to die? We can't live in this place. At least in Egypt there was bread and meat. It's better to live as a slave than to die in the desert. Are we any better off here than we were in Egypt?"

The biblical record reads: "The Lord heard the murmuring of the people and was displeased." You can understand why. After years of pleading, the Israelites had no gratitude for having received their freedom. They had no appreciation for the blessings of a new opportunity. The people wanted more, and the story suggests that the more they got, the more they wanted. With that perspective, how would such people ever be satisfied?

Is there any place in this whole universe where we can be happy if we are blind to our blessings and see only what we do not have? This was the problem of those long-ago people. They were not content in slavery, nor were they content in freedom. Nothing in the story suggests that they would have been content anywhere, not even in the "Promised Land."

After long and aimless wandering, the Israelites finally arrived in Canaan. Canaan was a rich land. As the biblical writers put it, "It flowed with milk and honey." But the Israelites were still murmuring even after they reached Canaan. They divided into factions, fought over their possessions, and squandered the riches of their new land in pointless disputes. They simply couldn't get things arranged to their satisfaction. It was a bad world everywhere they went. The story of these ancient people has been repeated a thousand times in history. It will happen again and again unless we recognize two things.

First, we must make demands on ourselves as well as on our environment. Part of the trouble with those long-ago people was this: they thought all their problems were environmental. In Egypt it was the slave drivers; in the wilderness it was the rocky, barren soil; in Canaan it was those troublesome Canaanites. There is no question that the environment was troublesome. The slave drivers were vicious, the wilderness was a tough place to live, and the Canaanites were not at all cordial to those wandering Israelites. But is it not true that there is something wrong with every place on this earth? Is there a spot on this planet where everything goes the right way?

Some of us never want to come face to face with reality. It's much easier for us to believe that we are at the mercy of the predetermined forces of heredity, environment, or biological urges.

Someone told about a young man in England who murdered his father and mother and then pleaded for the mercy of the courts on the grounds that he was an orphan. Absurd? Of course! But the alibi is the easy way out if it absolves us of responsibility and takes us off the hook. There is always one problem, however. When we live on alibis, every dream ends in despair.

It is reported that Ralph Waldo Emerson once wrote, "Henry Thoreau made last night the fine remark that as long as man stands in his own way, everything seems to stand in his way." If Emerson's insight is correct, escape from responsibility is impossible.

For many years Alcoholics Anonymous has had a phenomenal record in helping people. Somewhere in their literature there is a pharse, "The geographical cure." By this, the people of A.A. are referring to the therapy of changing locations. I do not remember hearing of anyone who managed to get his or her problem worked out that way. I do hear people who wrestle with such problems say this, "Sometimes we do need to move, get away from old surroundings, and find new associates. But until we are willing to determine whether the problem is personal or geographical, one place in this world is as good as another." That's a thought worth remembering. We will not find a new life here or on the moon if the problem is on the inside. The attempt to solve spiritual problems with geographical solutions is an impossible dream.

Will Rogers said that now and then he grew tired of the same old surroundings and would wish for a new place to live and work. He said that he would pick some city that sounded attractive. Before he moved, however, he would subscribe to the leading newspaper in his proposed new home and read that newspaper for thirty days. Rogers declared that he would always decide not to move. The news from where he planned to be was no better than the news where he was. Will Rogers was right. There is something right and something wrong about every place on this earth.

There is a second thing we must remember. Solving problems has a price tag. Those ancient

Israelites didn't understand this. They thought all they had to do was to wait for Moses to wave his magic wand and their troubles would be over. Moses had their new home all picked out. They thought their only responsibility was to climb into their chariots and ride away. No effort was needed on their part. That plan didn't work. Creation is so arranged that sooner or later, people have to pull their own weight. We are entitled to some help, of course, and to an opportunity to use what we have. But we can be helped only so much and be given only so much opportunity. In the end, problem solving gets personal, and there's no way to delegate it.

When Joseph Smith laid down the leadership reigns of the Mormons, the mantle fell on Brigham Young. Young knew that his people had been beleaguered and troubled. He heard that in Utah there was a desolate place known as the Great Salt Desert. Brigham Young took his people there, and they settled on the edge of that barren desert.

Today Salt Lake City is a place of rare beauty and contains one of the botanical wonders of America. There is a lesson here. The world of beauty belongs not to those who spend their lives looking for the ideal location. It belongs to those who dare to make flowers grow where they have never grown before.

Several years ago a radio station in the Midwest had an evening when listeners could participate in the broadcast. One listener with a quaint accent called in to make an observation: "Everywhere I go I hear people say they are trying to get away from it

61

all. I'm not," he said, "I'm trying to get into it."

That comment made me pause for reflection. The Promised Land is not necessarily just down the road or just over the next hill. Most often it's right where we are. If we can't find happiness now, we will likely never find it, even if we roam the farthest reaches of this universe. Happiness is not finding a place where everything is properly adjusted and all circumstances are exactly right. Happiness comes from working at those things that are wrong, like making flowers bloom in the desert.

A long time ago a Man lived in a remote corner of the earth. He lived only thirty-three years. So far as we know, he never traveled more than a hundred and fifty miles from the place where he was born. His homeland was one of the most troubled places on earth. He didn't try to escape, to get away from it all. He faced what was before him and considered every problem to be an opportunity. History has now rendered its verdict on this Man from Nazareth. No one has done better at life than he. Perhaps his example could bear imitation on our part.

Solving problems by changing geography seldom works, but facing up to life where we are can make living an exciting adventure.

*PRAYER:* O God of light and life, we sense a restlessness in our spirits that drives us to go to strange places and to do strange things. We yearn for peace of mind and heart that our days might be filled with beauty and joy. Teach us, Lord, that what we seek is not a place but a state of being. Help us see that unless we are right within, our world will always be wrong. Make us sensitive to the potential of the present and of the places where we are. Remind us, too, that you are everywhere; and where you are, we can find peace. Amen.

# Chapter 7

# THE TREASURES
# OF DOUBT

*Are you ever frightened because you have difficulty
accepting all you think Christians are supposed to
believe? Well, the truth is, you're not so different from
the rest of us. Most of us have seasons of doubt. The
question is, How can we deal with these seasons?
Read Judges 6:11-13.*

In 1925 the news media in America focused on a
small town in eastern Tennessee. A young school-
teacher named John T. Scopes was on trial for
teaching theories that some people believed were
contrary to the Bible. The principal participants in
the trial were two attorneys, Clarence Darrow and
William Jennings Bryan. Darrow had won a national
reputation for his skill in the courtroom. Bryan was a
three-time contender for the presidency of the United
States.

The trial attracted so much attention that years
later a movie was made about it entitled *Inherit the
Wind*. A scene in that movie portrayed a conversation between the two famous lawyers. Bryan stated
his belief in God and what he believed about God.

Clarence Darrow listened intently and then declared, "Mr. Bryan, the trouble with your God is that he is too high up and too far away."

Darrow's estimate of Bryan's thoughts may or may not be accurate. Nevertheless, many of us often feel that there is a great distance between God and ourselves. We like to believe that God is very close and that his concern for us is constant and real. But things keep happening to us that make us wonder about God's presence.

Sometimes we see our own reflection in the Old Testament story of Gideon, a faithful and devout leader of ancient Israel. For years Gideon believed in God's special providence and protection for the people of Israel. One day, however, the Israelites fell on troubled times. Gideon raised a pointed question, "If God be for us, why have these things befallen us?" There have been times when you and I have asked that question too. We want to believe that God cares for us but doubts keep creeping in on our faith.

Often our doubts bring with them a sense of guilt. We have been led to believe that faith is a virtue and to question it is both evil and wrong. Frightened by such thoughts, we attempt to stifle our doubts and ignore our questions. The trouble is, however, that doubt is like a steaming kettle—the more we try to suppress it, the more persistent it becomes. So how do we deal with our doubts? For many people that problem is acute. Young and old alike wrestle with it. Did it ever occur to you that doubt may not be a sin? Doubt can be a blessing.

Take a moment to consider the causes of our
doubts. Gideon's story in some ways parallels our
own. His people came to the Promised Land and
settled down to enjoy their new home. Far away on
the Arabian peninsula was a serious famine. The
people of that arid land began a fierce struggle to
conquer the rich resources held by Gideon's people.
To protect their crops, Gideon's people hid their
grain. An angel, so the record goes, spoke to Gideon:
"The Lord is with you." Gideon was in no mood for
sentimentalism. "Look," he said, "if God is for us,
why have these things befallen us? You don't have to
hide your grain when things are going well. If God is
on our side, why are we in hiding?" (paraphrase).

Gideon's problem is not greatly different from our
own. Often there is an inconsistency between the
historic affirmations of our faith and the situation we
presently see about us. The claims of our faith are not
always compatible with the hard realities of life. The
declaration that God loves us is contrasted with war,
famine, accidents, illness, and death.

Have you ever prayed earnestly for something you
believed to be good and right only to have that prayer
go unanswered? Have you ever observed someone
who least deserved it become the target of tragedy
and misfortune? Have you ever felt, as James Russell
Lowell put it: "Truth alone is strong; though her
portion be the scaffold, and on the throne be wrong"?
These are questions all of us have at times, and they
make us wonder about the validity of our faith.

It is possible, of course, to try to ignore such questions. Some of us attempt to do just that. There is a story in the Old Testament (I Kings 22) about a king named Ahab. Ahab was planning to go to war against a neighboring country. He called in his advisors for counsel, and they quickly recognized that the king's mind was already made up. He would tolerate no opposition, so the advisors gave the king a unanimous vote of confidence. But one of Ahab's colleagues sensed the insincerity of the advice and asked Ahab if there was not at least one honest person on his staff. "There is one," said Ahab. "His name is Micaiah, but I hate him. He never tells me anything good." Ahab's colleague insisted that Micaiah be summoned. Micaiah's report was not encouraging. "Ahab," he said, "your enterprise will not succeed. The war you are planning is wrong. You cannot win." Ahab ignored Micaiah. He locked Micaiah in the nearest jail and went about his war. But Michaiah was right. Ahab's course did lead to disaster.

We can approach our problems the way Ahab did. We can ignore our questions and stifle our doubts. That course, however, usually leads to trouble. Someone has said that most cynicism comes from people who try to live in an adult world with an infantile faith. Children think of God as a cosmic Santa Claus who doles out favors and gives us our heart's desires. Many of us never update that notion about God. We grow into adulthood still believing at kindergarten levels. Such a faith can't survive in an adult world. It only leaves us bewildered, confused, and cynical.

All of us know people who have suffered this fate. They are antagonistic and disillusioned about the faith. The problem, however, may not be with the faith but with their understanding of it. They may be trying to hold on to a childish notion of God that can't be sustained in the real world. It's a bad thing to ignore one's doubts. It's better to face them and ask the hard questions. Gideon did exactly that. He expressed his doubts in the presence of the angels and made no apology.

You see, doubt can be a friend to us. There are several reasons this is true. For one thing, our questions help us grow spiritually. Josiah Gilbert Holland once wrote:

> Heaven is not reached at a single bound;
> But we build the ladder by which we rise
> From the lowly earth to the vaulted skies,
> And we mount to its summit round by round.

Holland was right. We don't acquire heavenly things instantly. It's like becoming a mathematician. We start with simple addition and subtraction. Little by little our understanding grows until we are able to deal with the complex problems of algebra and calculus. Building a faith is not greatly different. We must take each precept of the creed, examine it, test it, and question it. We must struggle with contradictions and inconsistencies. But by constant study and prayer we take a step here and there. New insights dawn upon us and we find fresh glimmers of light. Great faith is always a growth process.

I have a friend who often says, "Never be afraid of a person who is asking questions. Fear only those who say they have all of the answers." That's sound advice. So often we are disturbed by young people who dare to challenge the most sacred ideas of our faith. Why should we be so fearful? Do we have a faith that will not withstand the honest inquiry of an intelligent mind? If the great ideas of religion are not sturdy enough to stand examination, can they survive in our kind of world? Honest questioning is often the beginning of a healthy faith. Instead of stifling such inquiries, we should encourage them.

Another reason for facing our doubts is that through this process our faith becomes our own. I saw an interesting sermon title once: "God Has No Grandchildren." I wondered if the theme of that sermon had to do with our attempt to acquire our faith "secondhand." That's a common pursuit among us. We examine the faith of others, study the creeds and read the Church Fathers. We know a lot about what others believe. That quest is helpful. It always widens our understanding to "rub" minds with other Christians. The time comes, however, when we must focus on what we ourselves believe if our faith is to have meaning. This requires the deepest kind of soul-searching and the testing of our conclusions in the laboratory of real life.

It's worth remembering that acquiring a faith not

only involves the establishing of a creed but also the confirming of that creed by experience. Recently I saw again that old story from the life of Blaise Pascal, the great French mathematician, scientist, and philosopher. He had lost a beloved daughter. A friend dropped by to visit and observed Pascal's quiet confidence and trust in the face of tragedy. Said the friend, "I wish I had your creed and then I could live your life." Pascal replied, "Live my life, and you will soon have my creed."

What we believe determines our behavior. It is also true that we act our way into believing. There are many intellectual difficulties in believing as a Christian, and some of the difficulties are as yet unsolved. But there are also difficulties in not believing.

It is difficult to explain the presence of evil with belief in God. It is equally difficult to explain goodness without a belief in God. You have to take a position and test that position in real life.

Confidence in God is best gained by living close to God. The more nearly you can follow God's will, the more nearly you can say with assurance, "I believe." It's a bit like getting to know a friend. The better you get to know that friend, the higher the level of trust becomes. The day will come when, despite what anyone tells you, you can say, "I know that person and I know what he will or will not do." People who set out to know God as a friend finally come to know God, and to know God is to trust God. Don't be ashamed of your questions. Out of your questions can come the greatest treasures of faith. When we have come through our seasons of doubt, we are able to say confidently, "I believe."

*PRAYER:* Almighty God, we want to accept the great promises of our faith, yet so often our minds are filled with doubts. We would like to believe that you are always with us, but the troubles and misfortunes we face make us wonder. Help us understand that while our questions are troublesome, it is through our questions that we can find our greatest assurance. Let us never be ashamed of our struggle to believe, for if we seek, we shall find. Give us now the strength to search for the truth, the wisdom to see it and the courage to act on it. In Christ's name. Amen.

# Chapter 8

## POWER WHEN
## YOU NEED IT

*Many people feel completely alone as they face life's
problems. The Bible, however, promises that God's
strength is available to us. Is that promise really true?
If so, how do we find that strength?
Read I Corinthians 3:4-9.*

Recently I read of a trial judge who imposed an
interesting sentence on a defendant before his court.
The defendant had been tried by a jury and the jury
had rendered a guilty verdict. When the judge
pronounced sentence, he said to the man: "I'm not
going to put you in our nice jail. I'm going to let you go
free and allow you to worry about taxes, politics,
unemployment, and the high cost of living just like
the rest of us."

Do you suppose the judge who pronounced that
sentence had had a bad day? To imagine that life on
the outside is tougher than on the inside requires a
different perspective from what most of us have.

It is true, however, that life anywhere has its
moments of suffering and hardship. A distinguished
American psychiatrist said in a lecture recently,

"Most people are up against it. When you strip away the masks they wear, you discover they have about all they can carry." Those of us who work with people are aware of that. The life of "quiet desperation" is a common human predicament. Young people struggle in a world where directions are not clear; parents wrestle with problems that defy human solution; older folk are troubled over shattered dreams and the infirmities of age; business and professional lives are filled with bewildering complexities. Problems are everywhere, and many of these problems seem beyond our power to handle.

Years ago someone coined a phrase, "God helps those who help themselves." No thoughtful Christian would ever quarrel with that. The apostle Paul once said that we are laborers together with God. What he meant, of course, was that our destiny is a cooperative venture with human and divine hands working in unison. How often we have emphasized this. Phrases such as "Trust God and keep your powder dry," "God favors the army with the largest battalions," and "Faith without works is dead" are common expressions. Sometimes, however, our insistence on the necessity for human effort leaves unemphasized our need for and the availability of divine assistance. God not only helps those who help themselves but also he helps those who *cannot* help themselves. That's a thought we need to ponder.

Many times we feel we have gone as far as we can go and done all we can do. With prayerful hearts we look upward seeking strength beyond our own. What hope do we have of finding that strength? Three thoughts have been helpful to me in trying to answer that question.

First, there is the biblical assurance that God can and will come to our aid.

All through the Bible, we run into this promise. One writer declared, "Cast your burden on the Lord, and he will sustain you" (Ps. 55:22). Another said, "Even though I walk through the valley of the shadow of death, . . . [God is] with me" (Ps. 23:4). Jesus said, "Whatever you ask in my name, I will do it" (John 14:13). Most of us have read these promises, but we often wonder if they are true.

Elton Trueblood in one of his lectures observed, "If you live long enough in this world to look back, you are going to see some things you can't explain except through the Providence of God." That's true, isn't it? The impact of Jesus on human history, for instance, has no other explanation. Every earthly force contrived to silence his voice. God, however, decided to keep Jesus alive forever. Jesus does live, and his kingdom covers the earth.

The persecution of the early Christians was designed to destroy the church. Instead, the blood of the martyrs became the seed of the church. The Romans built roads to bring the world under their domination, but the Christians used these roads to preach their gospel of deliverance. Paul was right. God works in all things for good.

What many of us see in history we have also discovered personally. Lincoln declared that he was often driven to his knees because he had no other place to go. There he found strength to carry him through some of the darkest hours in history. A lot of us share that discovery. There are moments in our lives when things appear hopeless. Yet doors seem to open and we find a way through. Our skeptical friends would have us believe that these open doors are coincidences, but those of us who have had such experiences remember Theodore Parker's observation: "The more I pray, the more frequently these coincidences seem to happen." God *is* willing to help in every time of need.

There is a second thought. The prerequisite for God's help is our willingness to receive it.

I once knew an unlettered man whose great wisdom more than compensated for his limited knowledge. One morning at the end of a service in his little church, he led the closing prayer. "Father," he said, "we don't ask for your blessings. Just help us to walk where your blessings are." What rare insight! There is little reason to pray for the sun to shine on us if we insist on living in the cellar. God's help is always given to us but we must be willing to receive it.

Harry Emerson Fosdick once wrote a book on prayer. In that book he told about a father who had a wayward son. The father knew the boy was headed for trouble and had tried to help him. His efforts were to no avail. Left with no alternative, the father stood by in pained silence as the stubborn boy ran his course. One day the boy came to the end. With all options gone, the young man turned to his father for help. "How I wanted to help you," declared the father, "but you wouldn't let me."

Please don't miss the point of that parable. The condition for God's help is surrender—a willingness to accept God's help. When Holman Hunt painted his picture "The Light of the World," his inspiration was a verse in the Book of Revelation. "Behold, I stand at the door and knock; if anyone hears my voice and opens the door, I will come in" (Rev. 3:20). Hunt painted the door to the human heart with no latch on the outside. God doesn't break down the door. Every person is the lord of his own house and heart. God gives us the right to live life our way. Only when we open the door and are willing to do things God's way can we receive divine help to get us through the problems and puzzles of life.

A third thought must be remembered. God's help often comes to us in ways we do not expect.

People who live in the Sun Belt shiver at the thoughts of winters where snow and ice are everywhere. They wonder how people make it when they are snowed in for weeks and spend days shoveling snow in subzero weather.

There is a story about a lad from the deep South who was drafted by the army. In the middle of winter he was sent to a base in the far North. After a week of battling the bone-chilling cold, he wrote home: "I'm glad we didn't win the Civil War. We might have had to occupy this country permanently." That statement was made in jest, of course, but it does suggest that our blessings are often disguised. We don't always recognize our victories when we are dealing with defeat.

God may lead us in unseemly places to get us where we ought to be. If you and I had been planning to bring a king into the world, we would never have chosen a manger. We would not have allowed his first visitors to be a band of lowly shepherds. Yet we now know that the very nature of Jesus' birth became the secret of his power. "God moves in a mysterious way his wonders to perform."

Someday when you have a few moments, read the Book of Revelation. You will discover a remarkable message. St. John is writing to the early Christians. "Look," he said to his comrades, "we are being persecuted. Pain and suffering are our lot. But don't lose heart. We are going to win. Out of our sacrifices, God is building his kingdom. That kingdom will survive when the proud Roman Empire has crumbled into the dust." John was right. The Roman Empire is gone, but God's kingdom survives.

God has a way of turning our failures and losses into victories. Hardship may not be removed, but we can find strength to bear and overcome it. The past may not be undone, but we can use it to make the future victorious. The world may not be calm about us, but we can find peace even in the storm. We may live under the sentence of death, but God will use the exit doors from this world as an entrance into a world where life is eternal.

It's a wonderful thing to know that we are laborers

together with God. It's even more wonderful to know that God is working together with us.

*PRAYER:* Father, sometimes we feel forsaken and lonely as we struggle with the events of life. Yet, you have promised that you will never leave us and that your strength will sustain us. Lift our eyes beyond the shadows of this world and let us see the light of your countenance. Help us understand that we are forever within your keeping. We cannot drift beyond your care. Amen.

# Chapter 9

# DON'T
# TRAVEL ALONE

*Have you ever wanted to get away from it all and leave*
*everyone behind? Most of us feel that way at times. But*
*friends are priceless treasures. They bring to life its*
*richest dimension. We really need one another. Take*
*a new look at the people around you. You*
*might find some unexpected treasures.*
*Read Ecclesiastes 4:9-12 (NIT).*

A few years ago a reporter for *Time* magazine wrote an article about one of the heroes of American history, Thomas Alva Edison. According to the article, biographers are now trying to sift through the stories and rumors that surround this man who contributed so greatly to the industrial revolution. The biographers of Edison are quick to admit his genius. They also suggest that he was an extravagant, profane, bull-headed show-off who circulated so many myths about himself that the historians have difficulty separating the facts from the legends. The new image attached to Edison is considerably less flattering than the one most people know (*Time,* October 22, 1979).

One thing that has become clear about Edison is that he borrowed constantly from the work of others. He claimed sole credit for the invention of the electric light. His own notebook, however, suggests that he leaned heavily on the work of Joseph Swan, an Englishman who had constructed a light using a fine carbon rod. Perhaps we should not be surprised at Edison's plagiarism. No one stands alone in this world, and few human achievements are solely the work of a single individual.

It is tradition in our land to glorify "rugged individualism." There seems to be some special virtue in making it alone. Our pioneer forefathers were always trying to get away from other people. They sought out new lands where they could exercise their independence.

Individualism does build physical, mental, and spiritual muscles. A long time ago, however, an ancient writer recognized the social need of human beings. In the biblical account of creation, the writer reports God as saying, "It is not good for man to be alone."

People are all around us, and in all of God's creation nothing is more priceless and precious than people. In our world we need one another. The author of Ecclesiastes sensed that. Listen to him: "Two are better than one. If one falls, the other can lift him up. If one is cold, the other can bring warmth; and if one is attacked, the other can come to his defense" (paraphrase, Eccles. 4:9-12). These are thoughts worth exploring. Never underestimate the value of

82

friends. Like diamonds, they bring a brilliance to life beyond measure.

Consider, for instance, our need for assistance from other people. Edison was not the only person who built on the labors of others. Most thoughtful people recognize their interdependence.

"Lefty" Gomez, an all-time great pitcher in American baseball, was once asked about the secret of his success. "Lefty" was not only a good pitcher, but also a very perceptive man. "The secret of my success," he said, "was a fast outfield!"

Charles Darwin openly admitted that the theories which brought him fame were based heavily on the thinking of the English economist and clergyman, T. R. Malthus. Einstein stated in later years that he stood on the shoulders of countless people.

The author of Ecclesiastes was right—two are better than one. He would have been equally accurate if he had said, "It's nearly impossible for one to make it through life alone."

The apostle Paul wrote many letters to his friends. In one of those letters he said, "Brethren, if one of you is overtaken in a fault, you who are spiritual should restore such a one in all prayer and supplication," (paraphrase, Gal. 6:1). The early Christians to whom Paul was writing may have found that instruction surprising. Most likely they expected him to say that if one of their number fell, that person should be removed from the fellowship of the church. The church must be kept spotless and clean. Paul, however, understood the frail dimensions of human nature and knew that all of us falter now and then. On such occasions we need help to regain our course.

Mountain climbers often tie themselves together when they scale high peaks. If one slips, the others serve as an anchor. In a very real sense, all of us are mountain climbers and most of us slip here and there. Fortunate is the person who has a friend to come to the rescue. Once in a while all of us need someone to help us up.

We also need one another for encouragement. There is an old legend in the church about a young man named John Mark. Mark's name appears in the New Testament in several places, and we believe he was a strong and vital force in the early church. If that's true, we almost missed his immeasurable contribution.

The legend, based partly on a New Testament record, suggests that in his early years, John Mark was an associate of Paul and Barnabas. At that time Mark was erratic and undependable. Paul became impatient with the young man. After repeated efforts to help Mark, Paul gave up and went on his way. But Paul's co-worker, Barnabas, thought he saw something in Mark worth cultivating. So Barnabas, whose name really means "son of encouragement," stayed behind and worked with Mark until Mark came through. Think about it. If the legend is true, much of John Mark's contribution we owe to the work of Barnabas. Barnabas found a young friend, stayed with him, and encouraged him. That young friend later held a vital place in history.

Countless people have made it through the rough places because someone walked beside them. Remember those dark days when the Romans set out to crush the early church. Christians were hunted like animals, arrested, and sentenced to die. In constant danger, how easy it must have been for them to lose hope. Those Christians, however, had a secret the Romans never understood. They met in the dark of night, in caves and on back streets. Together they reaffirmed their faith and commitment. Out of these meetings the Christians came with their nerves steeled and their courage renewed.

Have you ever heard someone say, "Why should I go to church? My religion is a very personal and private matter." There are selfish overtones to such a comment. The church not only gives to us but also it needs us. There are people in the church for whom we can be a source of strength and courage. Countless folk find life a lonely voyage. The presence of another traveler can make all the difference in the world. We *do* need one another.

The author of our scripture lesson also suggests our need for protection. "If one is attacked, the other can come to his defense." Are you ever troubled about the world of tomorrow? Can we possibly survive in a society where the spiritual and ethical teachings of Christ are lost? That has happened in a number of places on this earth, and not many of us want to live in those places. There the rights and dignity of human beings are ignored and the individual counts for nothing except as a pawn of the state.

It is becoming increasingly clear that only as the teachings of Jesus are taken seriously is there any hope for a just and decent world. If that is true, then the question remains, Can I keep Christ's name alive by working alone? When you consider that question, you are forced to the conclusion of a writer long ago: "Two are better than one!"

Clearly we do need one another. Because of that we should never take lightly the people around us. Our destinies are inseparably linked together. Our friends and neighbors are among our greatest treasures. They bring to our lives a dimension that nothing in all creation can ever bring. We must remember, however, that friendship is always a two-way street. As we give, so do we receive. "Reach out and touch someone." Bring a bit of joy, hope, and strength to someone who walks a lonely road. The day will come when you will travel a similar road.

When it does, you will find someone reaching out to you. If you have ever experienced that helping hand, you know the truth of the timeless proverb: "No one is rich who has no friends, and no one is ever poor who has someone who really cares."

*PRAYER:* Almighty God, how glad we are that we do not walk alone. Our lives are enriched by the friendship of those around us. So often they bring us light when we are in dark places, strength when we

are weak and hope when we are discouraged. Help us
not to take these priceless gifts for granted. Remind
us that such blessings have corresponding obligations. Let us, therefore, reach out to others, offering
to them our support and fellowship. Help us know
that if we have brought joy to one fainting heart, we
have not lived in vain. Amen.

# Chapter 10

# WHEN YOUR WORLD TUMBLES IN

*Have you ever wondered what you would do in a crisis situation? Suppose tomorrow a tragedy came to you or to someone you love. Is it possible to get ready for such circumstances? Jesus had a story that can help us find an answer to that question.*
*Read Matthew 25:1-9.*

A television station in the Southeast sponsors annually a physical fitness week for the community. As a part of the emphasis, the station brings to the area leading authorities in the field of health. Recently one of the station's guests was a woman who is a long-distance runner. The woman averages running eighty-five miles each week. During the interview the woman spoke at length on how to get started in an exercise and running program. Her first instruction was this: "You don't begin at full steam. The first few weeks you need to mix walking with running, and you should limit your exercise to a few days each week."

Those instructions make sense. We don't build physical stamina and endurance overnight. If that is true in the physical world, it seems reasonable that the same circumstances prevail in other areas of life. That may well be a part of the lesson in one of the parables Jesus told. He said that one day there was a wedding in which ten young women were to serve as bridesmaids. One of the responsibilities of the girls was to carry a small lamp they had prepared. Five of the bridesmaids took their duties seriously and prepared their lamps. The other five were not so careful. When the hour for the wedding came, the careless bridesmaids discovered that their lamps had no oil.

Jesus reports this conversation: "The foolish maids said to the wise ones, 'Give us of your oil, for our lamps have gone out.' 'No,' said the wise maidens. 'We cannot do that, lest there be not enough oil for you and us'" (paraphrase, Matt. 25:8-9). Those foolish bridesmaids learned an important lesson that night. There are some things in life you just can't get with only a moment's notice.

Have you ever wondered how you would react if you suddenly found yourself in a crisis situation? The crisis might be an accident, an illness, or even the death of a loved one. In time, such things come to most of us. If you have ever thought about what you would do in those moments, you may find some help in the parable of the ten bridesmaids. One thing is clear in this story. In times of crisis, what we are able to do depends a lot on prior preparation.

In Jesus' day, one of the functions of a bridesmaid was to provide light for the wedding feast. The time for the feast was not fixed. It began when the bridegroom appeared. The bridesmaids were to be ready at that instant. The people who heard Jesus tell the story understod this. Some scholars believe that Jesus used this story to describe his coming as the Messiah and the lack of preparation among his people to receive him. The story, however, has more extensive meanings. Life has a way of confronting us with emergencies. Whether we stand or fall depends on our preparation.

A former President of the United States was once asked for his secret to success. He pointed out that many times success depends on being at the right place at the right time. "But," he added, "the most important ingredient is to prepare yourself so that if the opportunity comes, you will be ready for it."

Both positive and negative implications are in our preparation for the unexpected. We may find opportunity knocking at our door, or we may be faced with potential calamity. John Greenleaf Whittier has a line in one of his poems, "I know not what the future hath of marvel or surprise." That's true for all of us, isn't it? We do not know what a single day will bring forth. We do know that all of us at times are called on to handle the unexpected.

For many of us the anticipation of the unexpected is a source of anxiety. To some degree, however, our behavior in a crisis situation can be predicted. What we do is partly conditioned by what we believe—our concept of God, our conclusions about right and wrong, our scheme of values, and the faith positions we have established.

There is an old story about a British commander who was sent to hold Gibraltar during a siege. Days went by and no word came from "The Rock." One day a messenger brought word to the commander's wife that the fortress had fallen. The wife's comment was, "Then Joe's dead." The woman didn't know what had happened, of course, but she did know her husband. She knew he would not surrender while he was alive. People are generally predictable. They act on what they believe.

Please remember, too, that inner preparation is an individualized process. The five wise bridesmaids refused to share their oil. Contrary to the way it may seem, the young women were not totally selfish. If they had given some of their oil to the others, they might not have had enough to last through the evening. The wedding party would then have been without any light. It wasn't a matter of selfishness. We have to do some things for ourselves.

I recall once hearing a husband say, "My wife handles the religion in our family." I have often wondered what the man meant. Was he saying that if the time ever came when he needed religion's answers to life's questions, his wife would provide them? If that's what he had in mind, he should know that it will not work. It's a bit like playing a musical instrument. We don't play a piano with someone else's talents. We must provide our own.

Inner faith is not an instant possession. The

apostle Paul admonished us to work out our own faith with fear and trembling—that is, give serious attention to what we believe. The day will come when how we stand up to life depends on the inner resources we have built for ourselves. We can't get those resources from someone else. They must be our own. It is this factor that suggests one of life's most important truths: every day we live, we prepare for the unexpected.

G. Ray Jordan tells of an old saint whose Bible was filled with notes written in the margin. Beside some of the verses the man had put the letters, "T.P." One day someone asked the old man what the letters meant. He responded, "Tried and proved." Nothing helps more in a crisis than the awareness that some things are tried and workable.

We are determining our response to the moment of crisis by the way we live every day. We really don't have a choice in the matter. Jesus once told about a couple of builders. One of the builders built his house on a shaky foundation. The other built his house on the rock. One day a storm came. One of the houses went down, the other stood. If you reflect on this story, you will see that it was not the storm that made the difference. The sturdiness of the houses was determined by the way the builders built them. Isn't Jesus saying to us that in one way or another, we are all determining in advance how we will handle the unexpected?

What a risk we take by neglecting this principle. We are so intent on providing for our physical security that we have neglected to build stamina in our spirits. We know how to provide food in time of famine, to give medical treatment in times of illness and to provide release from physical pain. But, we don't know what to do with loneliness, grief, and death. It's easy to be well-fed yet still have a hungry heart.

It is for this reason that we should give attention to matters of the soul. While our material treasures are important, even more important are the treasures of the heart. A day will come when whether we stand or fall depends on what we believe, on what we have "tried and proved." Fortunate, indeed, is the person who has made a decision about some ultimate questions: Does God exist? Does God really care about us? Does God answer prayer? Is death final? Is there a difference between good and evil? Those are decisive questions to consider. What you believe about them will make a tremendous difference the day your world tumbles in.

*PRAYER:* O God, there are times in our lives when we are confused and overwhelmed. Events crowd in on us in untimely and unexpected ways. We long for strength and assurance in such moments. Help us see that we can so prepare ourselves that when the storm comes we can rely on resources that come from above. In Christ's name we pray. Amen.

# Chapter 11

—•—

# DIAMONDS
# FROM THE PAST

*Do you ever struggle with guilt and anxiety about the past? How can we find release from the shackles of yesterday and be free to live life at its best? Read II Timothy 4:6-8.*

Can you remember times in your life when you stood at the crossroads pondering a decision you were compelled to make? All of us have faced such a circumstance, and in those moments life can be mighty lonely. Sometimes the decision is of little significance. You decide and go on with very little thought. On occasion, however, the choices have life-changing consequences. Perhaps the decision has to do with vocation, the choice of marriage, a business venture, or a moral judgment. Some people make such decisions and never look back. Others spend sleepless nights, wondering if the right choice has been made. The people who spend today worrying over yesterday lead tormented lives. We have to learn to live with the past if life is to have any meaning. How can we find the diamonds in the days that are already gone? The life of the apostle Paul, I think, provides some answers.

On the eastern coast of the Mediterranean Sea, once stood a city constructed by Herod the Great. This city of Caesarea, named in honor of Augustus Caesar, became the virtual capital of Palestine. Pontius Pilate, the Roman governor who presided at the trial of Jesus, had his official residence there. Among Pilate's successors in Caesarea was a man named Festus, whose only claim to fame was his association with St. Paul.

About nineteen centuries ago a trial was held in the court of Festus, and the results of that trial had far-reaching effects in history. Paul had been arrested in Jerusalem on a charge of civil treason. He was sent to Festus in Caesarea for judgment. But Paul, convinced that he would not receive justice in Caesarea, appealed his case to the emperor's tribunal in Rome. Paul's appeal to Rome may well have shortened his life. Subsequent investigation by Felix into Paul's case revealed that Paul's arrest in Jerusalem may have been unlawful, making a trial unnecessary. Paul, however, had appealed to Rome, and by Roman law once a case was appealed, charges could be dropped only by the emperor's court. While awaiting a hearing in Rome, Paul was caught up in the first waves of Christian persecution. Most people believe that he died a martyr's death.

Imagine how Paul felt during those final days in Rome. He must have known that the end was near, and that his own appeal for a trial in Rome had sealed his doom. But there is no record that Paul ever regretted his decision. Rather he said, "I have fought a good fight; I have kept the faith; I have done my best" (paraphrase, II Tim. 4:7).

Paul understood that very few people can boast of a perfect past. At best our yesterdays are filled with a mixture of good and bad. Any serious study of the lives of the saints makes this clear. So many of these great souls had checkered and tarnished beginnings.

We remember St. Peter, for instance, as one of the greatest of early Christians. There was a night, however, when Peter denied that he ever knew Jesus. Peter's denial may well have contributed to the crucifixion. Peter never forgot that night and often wished he could have erased his mistake. Augustine, in his early years, was so wild and undisciplined that his mother feared for his life. It's a rare person, indeed, who believes that he or she has consistently made the right decision and always taken the right road.

It is sometimes said that every human choice has both good and bad consequences. A few years ago there was a drama on television about a doctor in a midwestern city who had two patients suffering from a serious heart disease. One evening both patients became critically ill. The doctor had only the time and equipment to save one. He made his decision, knowing full well that one of his patients would not survive. This drama is repeated in real life time and time again. We seldom, if ever, choose between absolutes. Most often we leave behind a trail of good and bad.

Only the rarest of people live in this world without regrets. Not even St. Paul did that. He had some glorious achievements. During his journeys over the world he made many friends, and his life was brightened by the memory of them. There was Timothy, an exceptional force in the early church. This young fellow might have been lost for the church had not Paul taken an interest in him. Paul must have remembered hundreds of other people he had helped. But Paul's past had its heartaches. He had participated in the murder of Stephen, the first Christian to die for his faith. Paul never forgot his part in that dreadful deed. Years later in making his defense before Festus, he told of his terrible guilt about that. Paul's past was both satisfying and disturbing. Isn't that the way it is for most of us?

Have you ever received word of the passing of a friend and remembered something you had intended to do for that friend? Or what about opportunities you missed—opportunities that are gone forever? Sometimes I hear someone say, "If I could live my life over, I would live it the same way." I wouldn't! I would not do some things I've done, and I would do some things I have left undone. Most of us, if we are honest about it, feel the same way.

Reflection on the past, however, is of little value unless we use its experiences as reference points for the present and future. Sometimes I think our generation has an aversion to history. One of the complaints against the church these days is its preoccupation with the past.

A college student asked recently, "What do a bunch of camel drivers have to say to the space age? Why don't we quit talking about Moses and deal with the problems of the present?" I share that concern, but a total apathy to history can be dangerous. We cannot understand the present without some knowledge of the past. Carl Sandburg once said in a television interview, "Those nations that go down and don't come back are those that forget where they came from."

Every generation depends on the experiences and discoveries of the past. It is because of this that progress is possible. We don't have to keep reinventing the wheel, rediscovering fire, or rebuilding the electric light. We use the medical discoveries of doctors who worked decades ago. We add to their work and expand their knowledge. Behind every new technique are hundreds of discoveries, many of them centuries old. Knowledge is the accumulation of past experiences. It is risky, indeed, to try to live altogether in the present without some attention to history. It is good to reflect on yesterday if in doing so we are prevented from repeating the same mistakes.

There is, however, an unhealthy way to look at days gone by. Do you remember a cartoon a few years ago picturing a boy standing before the stationery counter in a bookstore? He was saying to the clerk, "Lady, do you have any blank report cards?" That lad's predicament is not hard to understand. A lot of us would like to go back to a few places and change the record. But the "time machine" exists only in science fiction. We cannot go back; the record stands as written. Paul knew that. Remember what he said, "Forgetting those things that are past, I press on" (paraphrase, Phil. 3:13-14).

The other night my wife and I were looking for a home we needed to visit. Neither of us knew exactly where it was. I had gone down two streets to a dead end. I remember that I had had the directions on a piece of paper and had thrown the paper away. I was lamenting my foolishness when my wife said, "Why don't we do something constructive?" "What do you suggest?" was my response. "Most people," she declared, "would stop and ask directions."

I keep thinking about that incident. A lot of us spend precious time worrying about the paper we have long since thrown away. We can't get it back by any human effort. The question we need to ask is what can be done under the circumstnces as they now exist. St. Paul understood this. He marked off what he couldn't do anything about and looked for what he could do where he was.

A basic principle is built into the scheme of things. God has so arranged his world that the past, no matter what it is, can be used for responsible and meaningful living in the present. There is a proverb which suggests a profound truth: "God never allows one door to close without opening another." Even a casual examination of history demonstrates this. No circumstance is hopeless. There are always open doors if we look for them.

Consider St. Paul. The Book of Acts suggests that if Paul had not appealed his case to Rome, he would have been released in Caesarea. During the proceedings there, Festus asked a fellow judge, Agrippa, to help him decide what to do with Paul. Agrippa heard the evidence and rendered his verdict. "I see no reason to hold this man. If he had not appealed to Caesar's court, we could release him" (paraphrase, Acts 26:31-32). Suppose Paul had been released and allowed to continue his work? How many more cities could have been influenced by his spoken ministry? We will never know because he was not released. We believe he spent the remainder of his days in jail. His travels were halted forever.

Even as the cell doors closed on him, however, Paul was thinking of another way to continue his work. From his prison cell he wrote letters, a practice he had learned years before. Some of those letters have been preserved even to this day. Those letters have probably had a greater influence on the world than his spoken words. When one door closed, Paul found another door open.

The truth illustrated here is the most marvelous hope ever proposed on this planet. Our lives are filled with sins, blunders, and mistakes. The gospel, however, is a message of deliverance. God is greater than our mistakes. He so arranges the past that the future is never impossible. Every circumstance is filled with the diamonds of opportunity if we look for them.

*PRAYER:* Father, the memories we have are not always pleasant. Sometimes our hearts are filled with guilt and despair. Help us remember that you are greater than all of our sins and mistakes. Let us forget those things that are behind us and look to the future with anticipation and hope. We claim your promise that nothing we have ever done need make the future impossible. In his name. Amen.

# Chapter 12

# THIS
# IS THE WAY

*For many of us life is drab and monotonous. Is that*
*what God intends? Jesus promised that living could be*
*thrilling and exciting. If that promise is*
*true, how can we find the way?*
*Read Matthew 7:24-27.*

I have a friend who spent the early years of his life in
a small rural town. When he was a boy his little home
church was visited by a whole parade of traveling
evangelists. These evangelists preached for a week or
two, usually on sin, which they rather vaguely
defined as the "appetites of the flesh." They always
seemed to be somewhat angry, and the more angry
they seemed, the more the people praised them for
preaching the gospel. Also, these preachers spent a
lot of time telling the people how difficult it was to be
a Christian. They urged their listeners to be faithful,
however, reminding them that for every pain and
difficuty they encountered here, they would be
suitably rewarded in the world to come. My friend
said, "I grew up with the clear impression that God
intended this life to be miserable. The more you

suffered here, the more likely you were to get to heaven."

Some of us have a similar notion. We believe we are supposed to suffer here so life can be good in the hereafter. How we came to believe this is something of a mystery. Jesus talked about the "abundant life." If we can believe the New Testament, the abundant life is both a present and future reality. Jesus did not mean that we could live without effort or escape the painful realities of this world. We are not created as finished products.

We are constantly growing and developing. Purposeful growth always presupposes resistance. Hills have to be climbed, hurdles have to be crossed, and problems have to be faced. The Good News of the Bible, however, is that we can master difficulty and not be mastered by it. Even more important, the Bible assures us that we can live in a world of conflict with joy, hope, and expectancy. Life can be exciting and thrilling even when the path is difficult. Jesus promised us that. The question is, How do we find that kind of life?

In the Book of Proverbs an ancient writer declared that as a person thinks in his heart so is he. This writer seems to be saying that if we can properly condition our minds, we can overcome anything. There is something to be said for this idea. If we can learn to live in faith and trust, a lot of the terror and apprehension in life disappears. But there is more to it. Jesus said, "Not everyone who says to me, 'Lord, Lord,' shall enter the kingdom of heaven" (Matt.

7:21). Jesus is saying that heaven here and hereafter are not just a way of thinking but a way of living as well. Or to put it another way, finding inner peace has to do not only with the way we think but also with the way we live.

God the Creator has an intended plan for life. One of the most remarkable Christians of this century was Dr. E. Stanley Jones. Dr. Jones roamed the globe working with people in every walk of life. A few years before his death, he wrote his autobiography, *A Song of Ascents*. In that book Dr. Jones said that during the last forty years of his life he never spent a single unhappy hour. Imagine that! Forty years of inner peace. Jones admitted that he had his shocks and sorrows but never for more than one hour had he been overwhelmed. Dr. Jones makes the thoughtful claim that there is a natural way to live; and when we find that way, we find ourselves.

As people of the scientific age, we shouldn't find that thought difficult to understand. We live in a universe which has a reliable and precise plan. Every star follows an exact path. If one star were to change its orbit, the whole system would be affected. The same principle governs the movement of the atom. We know, too, that our physical bodies are governed by certain principles related to food, rest, exercise, and the like. Why should we find it difficult to believe that there is an intended blueprint for our moral and spiritual lives?

Our forefathers talked a lot about the "will of God." They were trying to tell us that God wrote into creation the plan by which we must live if we are to find the abundant life. We are free, of course, to reject the plan, but we can never find the life God intended us to have until we accept his plan. How do we discover this plan? I think there are at least two methods.

The first method is by experiment. There is a story in the New Testament about a boy who decided he was too restricted by the rules of his father's house. The boy saw no reason for such rules.

One day he gathered all his father would give him and left home. He went to a far-away land and devised his own plan for living. If you read the story in Luke's Gospel you will discover how the boy's experiment ended. The prodigal son sat in a pigpen, a broken but a much wiser lad. He learned that the moral and spiritual laws he took so lightly were not the result of blind tradition. These laws were established in the plan of creation and were intended to prevail.

Isn't it interesting that all of our experimentation confirms the existence of these principles? A prominent attorney who recently addressed a large church gathering said that, in his opinion, if the Ten Commandments had never been written we would have by trial and error arrived at them. Truthfulness, for instance, is not a matter of custom, but it is essential for the survival of society. Respect for life is not just a romantic ideal; the foundations of our world demand it. That attorney is right, I think. One way to determine whether God's plan for life works is to try living the other way.

The second way to discover God's plan for us is by revelation. Many years ago a church school teacher in a small country town dramatized what he thought might have been the scene in heaven the day Jesus came to earth. He imagined God reflecting on his work with his children. He pictured God as saying, "I gave my people the Commandments, but they didn't understand them. I sent the prophets to explain the plan, but the people wouldn't hear them. I shall try one more time. I'll send my Son to show them the way."

That drama is an oversimplification, of course, but it does contain an element of truth. Jesus did show us the way. For two thousand years we have been examining the way Jesus lived. The verdict of history is clear: there is no other way to the abundant life.

God does have a plan by which he intends us to live. When we find it, we find ourselves. We can discover this plan by trial and error or we can accept what Jesus said. In any event, we always discover that the plan is there. Whether we accept or reject it does not alter its existence.

Why is it so difficult for us to accept God's plan for our lives? I have a friend who was a bomber pilot during the Second World War. His assignment was the South Pacific. Shortly after he arrived at his base he was sent to a class on jungle survival. "I slept through those classes," my friend declared. "I'd never land a plane in the jungle. I was too good at flying to do that." One night as he was returning home from a mission his plane was shot to pieces. The only place he could find to land was a small island two hundred miles from his base. When the plane slithered to a halt, the man said he looked back and saw his crew badly injured from the crash. "I realized," said the pilot, "that I knew absolutely nothing about living in the jungle. How foolish I had been. I had had a chance to learn how to live but I had slept through the classes."

Something akin to that is reenacted often in our world. We have a Book that tells us about a unique and special Man who lived a long time ago. His life wasn't easy but no one has ever managed to do as much with life as did he. He lived in a world of conflict, but he was always at peace with himself. He owned very little, but he now has a kingdom that covers the earth. He died deserted by his friends, but millions now give allegiance to him. This Man knew God's plan for life and lived it out for us. He proved that God's way to life is the only way.

All over the world people are looking for a way to make life an exciting and thrilling adventure. This search drives them to explore all kinds of intricate formulas and designs. Strange, isn't it, that so many of these people overlook the one example that endures every test of time? Jesus said, "I am the way." Those who have followed him learn that this is no idle boast or empty promise. They have discovered that heaven is not some distant goal but a present reality. In following Jesus, they find the life that God intended all of us to have.

*PRAYER:* O God, how glad we are that life is not an uncharted journey. There is a way to live with a sense of peace, joy, and expectancy. That way has been clearly marked by one who has gone before us. We listen now for his voice as it comes to us across the ages. We hear him say, "I am the way, follow me!" Help us join the countless millions who have heard his voice and taken him at his word. So let us live that each day may be a real adventure. We pray in the name of him who is the example for us all, even Jesus Christ our Lord. Amen.